PALACE OF SUBATOMIC BLISS

DARCIE DENNIGAN

CANARIUM BOOKS

ANN ARBOR, MARFA, IOWA CITY

SPONSORED BY
THE HELEN ZELL WRITERS' PROGRAM
AT THE UNIVERSITY OF MICHIGAN

PALACE OF SUBATOMIC BLISS

Canarium Books
Ann Arbor, Marfa, Iowa City
www.canarium.org

The editors gratefully acknowledge the
Helen Zell Writers' Program at the University of Michigan
for editorial assistance and generous support.

Cover photograph:
Alberto Giacometti, *The Palace at 4 a.m.*, 1932
© Alberto Giacometti Estate
Licensed by VAGA and ARS, New York, NY
© Man Ray Trust
Artists Rights Society (ARS), NY
ADAGP, Paris

First Edition

Printed in the United States of America

ISBN 13: 978-0-9969827-2-6

"now living 'alone' with them"

CONTENTS

THE STRANGER

Daniil Kharms was born twice.

That first time, they pushed him back in.

Maybe they can do that to my baby when it tries to come.

So don't have any children says the homunculus and not to get too stressed but I already have one and another on the way and he is serious. Very serious, serious.

More serious than I ever am, because his reality is phenomenal.

Mine's only noumenal. Case in point:

I'm driving to work. Supposed to be listening to a book on tape on Kant. But then I pass by a potato chip truck. The Utz truck.

Utz flavors: dill pickle, ketchup, Maryland crab.

And these are no boutique potato chips oh no.

Any gas station will sell you a bag for 99¢.

5:07 am

    1. If a baby can be born twice, then why oh why can't I?

    2. I am inspired by Le Corbusier to rechristen myself.

    3. Perhaps *La Bustier*.

    4. I will hereby be autonomous from logical thought, practicality, and everyday meanings.

    Signed,

    The Bra.

Panic.

And then the other day the homunculus says, What about "Sunshine" for the baby?

Camus' definition of the absurd having to do with the distance between the thing itself and the invented meaning of the thing.

"Sunshine" was suggested the day after the atmosphere's carbon levels had reached their blahblahblah, Canada was on the verge of becoming a jungle, the deciduous forests would all be deserts, etc. etc., he's telling me these things as I drive home from work, and the take-away here is that the homunculus wants to name the baby after the thing he thinks will kill us.

Let's call the little fetu "Camus."

What, and signal to the world that I had a baby instead of having a writer?

Kate doesn't get that joke.
That's okay.
It's not a great joke.

Are there female absurdists?

If there are not, I would like to be the first.

But I am suspicious as to why women have heretofore (if they have) eschewed it.

Have they realized something I have not.

THE BIENHEUREUSE MARGUERITE MARIE
(A FABLE)

I write to you from the cell of an anchorite.
I have lived here these past 13 years on potatoes, acorns, lice for
protein, and grass.
And I am very happy happy.

Am not leaving my cell.

Though very often my mother begs me to.

Marguerite Marie, she says, I am tiring, tiring of a diet of potatoes,
acorns, lice for protein, and grass.

My mother longs for pinot noir.
How is it that I've come to have such a bourgeois mother?

Potatoes, acorns, lice for protein, and grass! I bark.
And punctuate it with a kick to her stomach.

A letter to her from me, the Bienheureuse Marguerite Marie:

Dear Mother,
Pain is an eternal ingredient of the world's order.
To live a single day without suffering would be intolerable!
Nothing but pain will make my life supportable.
Signed,
The Bienheureuse MM

I have heard her explain her 13-year pregnancy very clinically:

"The subject may well find the outer world too full of shocks to dwell in."

Tralala! If she only knew how dry it is in here!
My suffering year to year increases.

Mother! I call up.
Yes, Bienheureuse Marguerite Marie?

Please swallow a hair shirt and an iron chain.

What, no potatoes, acorns, lice for protein, or grass? Hallelujah!
I will go slay a goat for its pelt straightaway.

And lice too, Mother. Lice too, to form celestial pearls on my hair shirt. And soap, so that I might worship with clean lips. Oh

Mother, I am so very happy happy at life's suffering thus far, and I've not even been born once yet!

But happiness ... in its way, is without reason, since it is inevitable.

Camus. Also he says humans only recognize fate in the face of tragedy, but that happiness is fated too. And therefore just as absurd.

I made the leap to that last sentence, actually. Might not understand Camus. You know, the *hormones*.

5:54 am

Check all that apply:

☐ Art and nothing but art. —Nietzsche (a paraphrase?)
☐ The absurd joy par excellence is creation. —Camus
☐ I prefer myself to eternity. —I forget
☐ I don't feel guilty asserting any of these things.
☐ I am lying.
☐ And, loading the dishwasher! Look how well the coffee cups line up. A job well done! Sisyphusean, thy name is woman.
☐ (Does anyone know what the feminine form of *idiot* is in French?)

Made great headway on my treatise yesterday.
Now cannot find notes.

One day, Albert Camus knocked on La Bustier's door...

Waving a telegram before La Bustier's face, he cried,
My mother has died!

Histrionics, proclaimed La Bustier
But she assented to Camus's request to climb onto her lap and curl up there

When her Thursday lover walked in, she quickly and expertly tucked
Albert Camus beneath her muumuu,
and, gesturing to the chair on which she sat, demanded of her Thursday
lover that their lovemaking occur in situ

Nine months later, Albert Camus was reborn
To the nurse who asked if she wanted to hold him, La Bustier replied w/ scorn

Yet before La Bustier abandoned her Camus baby altogether, she said:

You're lucky that you came to me on a Thursday, Albert Camus
Another day and my whim might as easily have been to kill you

... I'm sure this *is* a true story. Only, history has rewritten La
Bustier as a very busty & warm-hearted woman.

Absurdity:
The situation is compared to another situation, and the comparison
reveals a divorce

And now to a point!
But it's 6:SOMETHING.

All are awake. I am done.

—If the beings who inhabit this apartment swarm about me—they keep wanting their arms massaged and their mouths filled with specially roasted flax seeds—then I cannot write this treatise.

—And if I cannot write this treatise, then all I have in my head is panic.

—And if I'm alone looking out the window and the other beings from this apartment are away, then this treatise sits on my lap, and I look down and stroke the notebook's arm absentmindedly, and have an impulse to roast its pages, and panic is very good company.

—And the worst scenario is now! All are here, awake, in the next room, quietly pursuing their own aims, politely not a-swarm, and I miss them!

And I am panicked because soon they will leave and I will be blessedly alone.

And I will be alone.

—And now—I do not make this up—one is coming towards me—I am being entreated—oh hell—

Is the comparison of this situation to the one of a moment before the very definition of absurdity?

Shake if no, nod if yes—

I have no room to do.

This morning, peeking at the neighbor's paper, I found a photo of the poet Donald Hall with a cat in his lap, sitting on a chair very much like the one I'm sitting on now, only mine is, it's true, pink.

Instead of trying to prove in the abstract whether females can be absurdists, how about proving it by examples.

_____ (still thinking of good title):
An Anthology of Female Absurdists

featuring the work of

—

—

—Yoko Ono?

(must come back to this)

The nurse at the dr's yesterday: "Push this button every time you feel the fetus move."

If you say so.

Sartre: "All the sentences... equate to the same thing, as do all of the absurd man's experiences. Each one stands on its own and projects the others into the void."

If you say so.

3:54 am
The Russians: "The absurd is reality."
Me: *(She folds towels so that they are ready to be unfolded.)*

All exit.
Except the fish.

To file under: "Fuck This Stomach!"
At the coffee shop and can't find my wallet.
Must therefore empty bag and its unhygienic contents onto counter.
There's Queneau's *Elements of Style* with the tiny naked contortionists on the cover.

Counter girl coos: *Oh, is that a mommy & baby exercise book?*
Could her voice be any louder.
FTS!

So the fetus did try to come out early.

I was able to stuff her back in and help her regain fetus status, but not before she made a few requests:

—She would like to be Russian

—She would like to be male

—I am to remember that she can hear me talk and thus stop interjecting inanities for the duration

—For example, she elaborated, when watering the basil plant, she prefers that I not say loudly and brightly to absolutely no one, "Basil!"

Going to pop this treatise out by Tuesday.

Daniil Kharms hated children.

<u>petite play</u>

scene: a woman's prison

woman 1:   What are you in for?

woman 2:   I was raising my child in a meth lab.

woman 3:   I sold my child to a migrant farming family.

woman 4:   I told my child that the mold on her corn on the cob wasn't really mold and she ate it and died.

woman 2:   Did you get your refund on the bad corn?

woman 4:   No, store credit only. I used it to buy some cucumbers.

woman 1:   What big cucumbers they sell in stores nowadays!

… the end.

Remembering the disgusting moment at the faculty dinner as we all took our seats when I felt the need to announce to nobody in particular, "I'm starving" ("Basil!") and the male professor gave my stomach a significant look and said, "You must be."

No, buddy, there was no inner meaning there.
There's no inner meaning anywhere.

Numero uno obstacle to becoming a female absurdist: because one harbors, in a central region, ovaries, feti, etc., people are always presupposing one's utterances have an inner meaning.

5:44 am

You are all very lovely
I have no specific qualms with any of you
Here let me fold you a towel so that you can unfold it
I need time to think please don't give me time to think
The goldfish in their bowl
Mon Tues Wed Thurs Fri
Divorce, discrepancy
The stage set collapses

Here's what I've figured out so far.

You can skip this page.

(YOU CAN SKIP THIS WHOLE THING.)

The French absurdists	Perceive facts but do not grasp their meanings for there is no meaning to grasp
The Eastern European absurdists	Perceive facts but do not grasp their meanings though there are meanings, distant and inexpressible, to grasp
The Russian absurdists	Perceive facts but want to kill their meanings with error & accident, for perhaps there is some (Interruptions from other humans since trying to finish this sentence: two) for perhaps there is some (three!) (on the verge of four) (moving on)
The would-be female absurdists	What big cucumbers they sell in stores nowadays!

early

The fetus is now 3 lbs. If it tried again to be born today it most likely wouldn't die.

I mean it likely would not die *right away*.
Obviously I'm sitting here gestating something that will eventually die.
(tralala, doing so it can be undone)
(Viz: The towels.)

With a major weather catastrophe imminent, the homunculus thinks it would be tidier if the fetus just stayed inside so that the same flood or fire that kills me can simultaneously wipe out the fetus.

etc.

<u>The #1 Female Absurdist</u>
a petite story by The #1 Female Absurdist

Once a female had a pen in her hand and a notebook in her lap
and a fetus in her uterus and a homunculus in her apartment
and a child on the arm of her chair and No! The child did not ask
her a question about life's meaning.
The child said nothing important.
There was a coffee stain on the windowsill.
And what else?
Some packets of flower seeds.
But they're not important.
Nothing is important here.
And nothing happened this morning.
Except that I changed chairs.
Now I am in the corner
to make it harder for the apartment's inhabitants to see me.

... is what she wrote.

<u>The Solution Is Out of the Question</u>
And now he's offering to make me eggs.
That is very nice, so nice, he's sweetness almost all the time.
As a matter of fact I'm starving.
Eggs would be wonderful!
And with spinach too! I certainly need the iron.
But I've shaken my head before the offer was even out.

1. I too closely resemble an egg to eat one without an all-
   consuming self-consciousness.
2. Feed me, love me, leave me alone!

Found an index card with some treatise research in the cushion of
this pink chair:
*"When it is absolutely necessary to allude to a preceding sentence, the
author uses words like "and," "but," "then," and "just then," which evoke
nothing but disjunction, opposition, or mere addition…*

And found some unchewed gum.

—Must wash clothes for impending fetus.

—And if the fetus pends too early and dies, how absurd will this task of laundry seem then.

—How many men have I dated who quoted: "There are words that mean nothing. But there is something to mean." Damned beard-support systems.

—I want to be free, dear blessed necessary entanglements;

I cannot write with interruption;

Interrupt me;

The wind came & blew apart the clothes' neat folds;

Mon Tues Wed Thurs Fri Mon Tues Wed Thurs Fri;

But two more Mondays would mean the fetus could be born undangerously;

But the homunculus is charting three more Mondays till the apocalypse;

But;

Fuck this stomach;

Anthologies of work by female writers who write about having children, I also detest;

Bo-ring says The Bra;

I like only flowery plants;

Have you seen my neon pink maternity wear;

Did you know that basil plants flower;

I...;

Elements of the Hittite!;

—It will be hard, in this new neighborhood, to walk around with ahusbandandtwochildren;

I love them very much and what nice old trees here and how mortifying.

—If we could all cut off one leg each and then limp around the block *that* might save us from such mortification.

—Or if I lost them all in a senseless accident

—Or if I lost them due to the perfect cause & effect of my own personality defects

—Then I could walk around this neighborhood with a perfectly preserved sense of self

Tuesday, 5:something

The fetus has submitted a list of utterances she might make upon the occasion of her birth.

The list was pushed through my naval in an envelope soaked with amniotic fluid and marked, "For your consideration."

1) Plaudite, amici, comoedia finita est

2) Cease! Suffering is irremediable

3) At first a little joy, then a chain of sorrows

4) *Maman died today*

5) Thus begin I hunger, sex, and the succession of day & night

6) Thou mayest no longer be a man, not for thyself, only for others

7) The solution is out of the question

The goldfish watch me.

My rants, my handwringing, the senseless mimicry with which I dress, coffee, drive to job, laundry, murmur to other humans— all from behind my glass retaining wall. I am absurd to them.

If someone would explain to me the difference between a swallow and a sparrow, I would let the rest go.

That solution is out of the question.
The solution has left the question.
Exit, the Solution.

WATER FOR SALE

I am always washing things

(I'd make a list here but my hands are wet)

This morning washed a fish who'd leapt its bowl

from the floor. I am always washing

things, and washing the fish from the floor what flooded

my thought: *we perish'd, each alone.*

Hands always busy at the tap, can carry no thought

to the extreme "... *but I beneath a rougher sea,*

and whelmed in deeper gulfs than she..." all day

I listened to that deep water and wanted to

swallow all of it or be swallowed by it

(I did, was) (do! am am am) When do I get

to say to myself, *That's enough, you can stop now*

Instead of the stupid dogged paddle I'm peddling

That's enough. You can shop now.

serum factum

(I wrote this with one finger in the steam on the glass)

I made this water so that I could know it was true

or,

I made this water a metaphor so that I could know
what was true

am terrified to go back and read this in case I
hear (between waves of thought) {   }

The problem of selling puddles

is how to package them

If I put this puddle in a glass bowl

(yeah?) wouldn't it cease to be a puddle?

Quite moist, these problems (oh yeah)

I'm alive as—

what—

(I want to buy a Great Lake!)

If I were alive

to the truth of my life would I (not) be

dead? I feel this urgency in my being

(a Great Lake!)

and also an urgency to retreat from the surface of action

that the first urgency brought me to

alive/dead, the surface tension interrupted

by swells

(a Great Lake, please!)

The swells together making one Hesitancy

All's well

Just swell

Something happened to me, that I, because I didn't

know how to live it, live as something else

How much is it worth?

What? This pool deck furniture of a woman's mind?

(And there's the sales tax!)

Tithes of mintwater and anisewater and cumminwater—

etceterawater—

You asked how much is it worth

Were I to name the price the price would be my name
(Would I name the price if the price were my name)

Fish on the floor, gasping in the chiasmus

(How can I be sure it is I I am selling it to?)

There's water on both sides of the scale

Something *happened.*

(Sorry to have to say it again.) (Swimmer's ear.)

Let every thought be drought

I know only in order not to know

Consciousness is not a biological process

I await someone who does not share my lungs, etc.

This shoppe is a better world than I deserve

There is so much light here

When I decided to enter the forest of water I knew

it would be dark, and isn't it just like me

to find all the phosphorescence

(plus an underwater speaker for synchronized swimmers)

isn't it just like me to find a clerk job

in the inner world to keep busy

Let every drought be sought

Froth is a dream (Calderon)

Thirst is such stuff as dreams are made on (Shakespeare)

—I'll buy that second one

as a bumper sticker for my paddle boat

because if dreams are poured on top of thirst then

desire for water is the ground I sleepwalk on

or if water's only a dream that dreams up itself

the word *dream* is rinsed of its weight

… thrashing around in the rhetoric (notwavingbutdrowning)

What's the return policy on soggy items?

The only words I want are the ones I do not know

I would like a foothold in the actual world
Then behold:

This glacier, which you must crest
before it defrosts

(the only thing that interests
me is whatever cannot be
thought whatever can be
thought is too little for me)

… you know what
you can't buy this glacier

here's a straw

here take a sewer bill
and a straw

(I love living!)

here drink this can of fluoride
and you will have died

To keep myself busy I've been re-arranging the shelf

of surfaces and there are many—shores, docks, piers,

wharves, poolsides, beaches—my hands're wet but see how busy

my mouth is, declaiming? I cannot talk

brightly, lightly (loud!) enough to the customers

to stop this fear (I can almost hear

the message I do not want to hear)

Now I'm splashing vigorously to drown it out

(See my hands at work? "splash" "drown" etc.)

(i.e., I refuse to doff the bathing suit my words wear)

(i.e., This page is a no-nudes beach)

Eighteen thousand times the poor messenger has chased me

through the little underwater castle of the fish bowl

while I, to escape her, have climbed (vigorously!)

up the minaret and thrown myself off

I can only conjecture from what has passed so far that this play's outcome will contain a sadness that will at first feel buoyed by surface sadnesses but whose very surfaceness will belie a deep tragic sadness, like peering too long at a portrait whose aim was to produce a likeness of a real woman but for whose model the artist used a doll (all day I am washing the water-globed jewels, swabbing the shark reef). Either a malignancy is inside me or I am inside a malignancy (busy busy busy!) (hello welcome to the water shoppe, how may I help?).

Self-belying, I said but I heard *self-bellying* and

if you're trapped inside the whale you must sell the belly!

the packaging has got to be spectacular!

or this fish business will really go belly up!

now that I've gotten rid of that belly I'm bikini-ready!

sold it for a song, got soaked in silence

etc.

That is an ache and *this* is a distant numbness

If in the shoppe this happened and in the actual world that

happened, what is the message? I would like to meet you

before you die. I think I will have to die to meet you. You

are invited! It is I who invites you. Of course it is I who I

am inviting, and since that's true, you know how

(how much?) I want to hear from you

Have read one book: the one from which I drew this water

Have watched one station: the one with apophatic

simulations of gone seasons (How dost the cosmos

as it nestles in my particular breast?) This brittle mask that

cannot reflect the face, its happiness, upon prying

open the submarine hatch and reading the neat tiny hand

of the drowned one's note that has yet to be written

I do not not want to meet you

(I love living!)

But you come all of the time, here you are again

I would like to buy a bell

Very well, very well

And you're looking at me and I am looking away

With my apron on I sell you the sight of an eddy

With my apron on I promise you that

when the eddy is frothing, it means that in the other world

a bell is ringing—you can be sure

Though I sell more doubt than certainty

Though

(I am of course knowingly continuing to talk so that you can-

not) my greatest fear is being

The eddy is frothing

The bell ringing

being being being

THE PALACE AT 4 A.M.

The authorities come, in the middle of the night, on ignoble steeds, to take Hannahbella away.

They come to take her away and they took her away, but she remains, for I have built this palace for her on the 13th, and therefore nonexistent, category of reason.

They come to take her away and they took her away, but she is still here rehearsing her walk off the tiny plank. And there she is again, begging our prehistoric bird for another ride around the rotunda.

But here are the authorities, coming on their strapping steeds, to take Hannahbella away.

They took her away, and their stomping upset our fragile beams, and we, Hannahbella and I, have been left behind to right them. We right them like spines, one after the next, up four floors of the palace, and then together Hannahbella and I walk the roof wire and right the spire.

Now the palace is becoming crowded. There is Hannahbella, and there is I, and there are also all the Hannahbellas who have been taken away, who are also still here, in cages suspended from the palace's high ceilings.

They come to take her away and they take her away and the palace is peopled with Hannahbellas, each rehearsing a different scene cut short from the life of Hannahbella.

And one of the Hannahbellas rehearsing a scene from adolescence asks me why, if I am such a believer in effacement, why do we live in a glass case where all can see our movements? And they come to take her away and they take her away and it is very difficult for me for I miss terribly even this most belligerent of Hannahbellas, who, a teenager of terrible grace and anger, has been left behind and is lighting the palace on fire.

(But Hannahbella, when they take you away the palace grows rooms, rooms, there is so much room in here to think, such large rooms, Hannahbella, I am not exactly sorry to have.)

The townspeople are coming out to watch the palace glass shatter, to watch my Hannahbella pour cold piercing light all around her. A shard may have struck me from above, but I am busy, very busy, because here are the authorities charging in on shining steeds to take away all the Hannahbellas in existence, all the real ones and all the memories of what was real and all the memories of what about her was not real but still exquisite, which means that of course they must take me too, for it is I who keep insisting that the fragile princess exist.

They come to take me, the queen, but I am cleft in two, and when at first they do not know which of me to take, I announce to them a riddle I think may spare me:

Do not despair; one of the queens is saved. Do not presume; one of the queens is damned.

But they took us both.

DANDELION FARM

WHEN I WOKE
THE PIANO WAS THERE
BESIDE ME ON THE LAWN

That was the first line of the play.

I remember a note in the script.
The stage is a beautiful and real lawn. The lawn must be the length *of sleep and the width of the greatest distance the ancients could imagine: a solo voyage from Cyprus to Corsica.*

Later on somewhere I read that the playwright and set designer were lovers.

The stage is a beautiful and real lawn.

PHILIPPINA unrolls a length of sod the size of a gravesite and lays down.

ANNOUNCER:
FUNERAL!

The ENSEMBLE blow white dandelion puffs onto the body.
A CHILD gives a eulogy.

CHILD:
SORRY YOU HAVE TO GO SO SOON.
SORRY YOU HAVE TO GO SO SOON!

The ENSEMBLE, singing along with Mahalia Jackson and Dinah Shore
to "Down by the Riverside," toss the stripped stems onto the body and exit.
The last one to leave is the actor playing the CHILD.

CHILD:
AS CHILDREN, NO, WE NEVER WERE ABLE TO TAKE OUR MOTHER TO THE PARK.
WHEN CONFRONTED WITH AN EXPANSE OF LAWN, SHE IMMEDIATELY
BEGAN TO PERFORM A PART IN A PLAY. THE PLAY, SHE SAID, WAS CALLED
DANDELION FARM.
NEITHER MY BROTHER NOR I HAVE EVER BEEN ABLE TO FIND A RECORD OF
A PLAY BY THAT NAME.

There was a play, and I had the first line.

PHILIPPINA:
WHEN I WOKE, THE PIANO WAS THERE BESIDE ME ON THE LAWN.

I remember I was to say that line at the edge of the stage, which was really a lawn.
Or at the edge of the lawn, which was really a stage.
I was to say it directly to you, as if you knew what I was waking from.

PHILIPPINA:
WHEN I WOKE, THE PIANO WAS THERE BESIDE ME ON THE LAWN.

I was to speak the line at the edge. I looked into the dark and felt so much like Philippina that I forgot to feel like myself. And Duke Ellington's "Black and Tan Fantasy" was playing.

When we were first married, we didn't know where to live.
It had to be cheap but beautiful,
but of a heretofore mostly unremarked beauty, because it had to
be cheap.
We wanted seascapes of empty space, but also busyness.
To be packed in among daffodils, or among people who lived like
daffodils...

him: How about carnations? Would you take carnations?

me: But they are mealy-mouthed flowers, they are milky, no I
cannot take carnations.

(there was a delicate pause)

me: If we cannot live amid daffodils, I could concede—I could
take delphiniums.

him: Delphiniums! Delphiniums are worse. so dark. too delicate.

(a more delicate pause)

him: Shall we start a dandelion farm?

The poster advertising the play had a photo of a lawn from a dream, and on it the whole ensemble, sunbathing.

In the middle of the lawn, where the spotlights shone strongest, was the player piano.

To the right of the piano was a platform, two feet high, with three rickety steps leading up to it. On the platform was a microphone, and an announcer in an oversized suit put his mouth right on it.

ANNOUNCER:
THUS BEGINS 200 DAYS OF ORDINARY TIME.

That was our cue, the ensemble and I, which was made of women and children and gay men, to commence silent picnicking, croquet, circle dancing. The Merseybeats "Mr. Moonlight" was playing.

ANNOUNCER:
THUS BEGINS 200 DAYS OF ORDINARY TIME.

Then the ensemble would begin zigzagging across the lawn, barefoot. They were always dancing to a song that was a little faster than the one blaring from the player piano's invisible speakers.

At the end of the song, I, as Phillippina, was to separate from the group.

PHILIPPINA:

I AM TI-ERRD. I AM TI-ERRD.

I was to go off to the edge of the lawn again, lightly, like a silk handkerchief, though I remember the edge of the lawn feeling like the lip of a bridge.

From the middle of the lawn the ensemble called to me.

ENSEMBLE:

SORRY YOU HAVE TO GO SO SOON.

ENSEMBLE:

SORRY YOU HAVE TO GO SO SOON.

At home after rehearsals I would ask my husband if I could jump off something and have him catch me.

me: Please, I need to know what's at the other end of the jump.

him: We live on a lawn. the tallest thing we own is a dandelion.

me: I could leap. i could run and leap up and you could catch me coming down.

----

him: I'm sorry i dropped you. my arms are weak.

me: We can pretend it never happened. That way I'll still be able to insist you are strong.

We went to sleep and I dreamed that he promised to plant a tree that would grow to enormous heights.

And as we slept, the actors from the ensemble would come to our lawn and play pyramid games.

GREEN COWBIND AND MOONLIGHT*COLOU

The play, I remember, had such length that often, during a blackout, they had to replace the child actor who had grown too old on the lawn blowing dandelions with a new child actor who was young enough to play a child on a lawn.

The last line of the play was the child's.

CHILD:
SORRY YOU HAVE TO GO SO SOON. SORRY YOU HAVE TO GO SO SOON.

I remember the director had the hardest time making sure the child didn't sound mournful. She would yell at the child from the darkness:
Lightly!
Brightly!

CHILD:
SORRY YOU HAVE TO GO SO SOON. SORRY YOU HAVE TO GO SO SOON.

My own children would say that all the time to me when I was just going a few yards away to collect myself.

<u>characters</u>

-*ACTRESS WHO PLAYS THE PART OF PHILIPPINA*

-*PHILIPPINA (played by the same person as above)*

-*ACTOR WHO PLAYS THE PART OF THE CHILD*

-*CHILD (same person as above)*

-*DIRECTOR (female, and older than actress who plays Philippina)*

-*ANNOUNCER (elderly and very skinny man)*

-*ENSEMBLE MEMBERS, WHO PLAY THE PARTS OF "HE," "STAGEHAND," AND OTHERS*

The bugs have eaten many pages of the original script, but that was the cast page.

My parents, the story goes, had a hard time making money.
They flit around the city.

People offered them desks, chairs, paychecks but my mother, she wanted to be an actress and needed to be free to audition in the afternoons.

My father wanted to be an umbrologist and needed daylight to catch the best shadows.

They decided to live in the park. My mother had always acted as if she were on a day-long picnic.

At night, my father hid them both under his shadow collection.
They were clean always, impeccably clean always.

What is the phrase I always remember—or forget.
Look your last on all things lovely...?

Even dandelions, it turned out, were practical.
We were arguing with trowels in our hands.

him: Gram for gram, they have more vitamin a and d than corn.
me: But I don't want to grind or mill them.
him: But you are always asking to lift things that are heavy.
him: You are always waking and asking if you are here.
him: Imagine the weight of the mill wheel. Imagine the noise of the
dandelion tumult pinning you to—

me: What if we braid the stems together like lanyards
me: What if we—
me: Yes! What if we made pillows out of dandelion down.

him: Yes.
him: Yes, quickly, let's stuff the down into the fabric, quick now—

her: Festina lente!

That was what the director used to say to us during the dance
scenes.

me: We could dance right now

him: I'd rather lie down.

Then we went to sleep. The night fast-forwarded. In the morning, a fountain woke us.

Am I still here? Why am I still here?

ANNOUNCER
ECLIPSE PARTY!

It was a 100-year scene that was to be played in 3 ½ minutes
without hurrying.
Tia Blake's "Plastic Jesus" wasn't very loud but it was always there
in the background.

At one point, the ensemble was to whip out smoked glasses, don
them, look toward the sky, and quail.

I was to walk the length of the greensward to the proscenium's
edge and alone, narrate the eclipse.

PHILIPPINA:
THERE ARE GREAT BLUE SPACES AT THE BACK OF US
AHEAD: A SCRUMBLE OF RED AND BLACK
BACK AGAIN, AT THE BLUE
NOW NO COLORS
NOW THE LIGHT SINKS

ENSEMBLE:
THIS IS THE SHADOW! THIS IS THE SHADOW!

The children, dressed as sheep, were to pretend to eat the grass.

PHILIPPINA:
THIS IS THE SHADOW. NOW THE LIGHT IS OUT. WE ARE EXTINCT. THE

EARTH IS DEAD. WE ARE FALLEN.

Then the stage lights were to go off.

this is page 37 of the original script:

The lights are up in the house. Some lights go back up on the lawn, but they look flat instead of sunny.

A STAGEHAND with clippers clips the lawn.
There's the slice of metal sides passing each other.
This goes on for a few minutes.

Then the stagehand gets up on one knee.
He surveys the grass.
He says something to the effect of, "Good enough for the matinee."
He leaves.

It would be dark when I came home from the theatre.

me: Are you here? Will you help me rehearse?

him: I'm in the other shadow.

me: Will you help me rehearse? I have to die.

him: How

me: The stage direction says, "she jumps"

him: Into what

----

me: I could stand on your shoulders.

— Steady—Ready?

me: "If I hallo'ed your name to the reverberate hills…"

he laughed at me

me: "If I hallo'ed your name to the reverberate hills…"

him: Is that really the line?

I stood on his shoulders for a long time. I could see so far into the distance that I didn't recognize myself anymore. Or rather, right as I did finally jump, I saw another, private self I'd never met before, and though time was still a very long and wide thing, it was no longer an endless green pavilion and as I fell, I wanted to stay on the grass undrowned but always almost-drowning, desperately, happily, *just a*bout-to-drown.

PHILIPPINA's voice over the loudspeaker:

"YET I AM NOW AND THEN HAUNTED BY SOME SEMI-MYSTIC, VERY PROFOUND
LIFE OF A WOMAN, WHICH SHALL ALL BE TOLD ON ONE OCCASION..."

I would walk the lawn, picking dandelions, mouthing Philippina's
line, trying to memorize it.

Once, he came up behind her as I bent to pick a stem.

I knew he was there.

"YET I AM NOW AND THEN HAUNTED"

I stopped.

We were very close.

There was a great invisible screen separating us.

And then the screen, when it broke, broke one thread of metal
fiber at a time.

DIRECTOR: ENEMY! VIOLENCE! BRUTE!

(But on the whole the love scene was very gentle.
He picked some dandelion fluff out of the knot in my hair. And
then he wandered away.)

The voice over the loudspeaker the whole time:
"YET I AM NOW AND THEN HAUNTED BY SOME SEMI-MYSTIC, VERY PROFOUND
LIFE OF A WOMAN, WHICH SHALL ALL BE TOLD ON ONE OCCASION..."

I don't remember whether or not this was a scene in the play.

WHAT CAN BE MADE FROM DANDELIONS:
SALAD
WINE
CHILDREN
UDUNUM LAUDUNUM   JM

Am I still here.

I remember waking up on a lawn and beside me a piano was playing... Debussy?

And there was an old playbill taped to the side of the piano. It had a photo of a lawn from a dream, and on it the whole cast, sunbathing.

I recognized the lawn I was lying on as the lawn in the playbill.

The lawn must feel like an endless green pavilion. The grass, nostalgic.
The horizon, dangerous.
In the green of life enisled, with echoing straits between us thrown.

Ensemble member:

She got married and went away. None of us saw her anymore. Then the director had a party one night, a great party, a cast reunion, in a park. She had laid all these bright towels out—yellow ones, and turquoise ones and orange-y ones. It was late, but she had rigged up some stage lighting right on the lawn. And I ended up being the disc jockey. She just had 45's, and a strange collection too, so I was pretty busy trying to keep some kind of music going. She had some Highway 61. She had Rolf Lisveland's Tourdion—on a 45! She had Ward Swingle doing "It was a lover and his lass."

We were all there—everyone from the play—Angie and Vi and the swizzle stick musicians and Kit and his whole crew and even the kids who had played the child, only now none of them did really seem like kids. And Philippina showed up and she'd already tried to kill herself and they had rescued her and we'd all heard about it. And there she was. We hadn't seen her in a long time. And she was going around to each towel, kissing each one of us, in a light way but also with a smack, and she started doing, "I've got to go," and she was just going to leave, and I walked away from the record player and started trailing her around the rooftop saying "Going to leave?" It felt like she was going to really leave forever.

And then the record stopped. It was quiet for a minute—everyone was sort of half off their towels—like when a lifeguard at the beach blows the whistle and the sunbathers rouse to see if it's a shark, or drowning. And we looked at each other, all of us. And we picked up Philippina and started carrying her around. We carried her up and down the lawn, around the park perimeter, for a long time.

Then Kit and his group carried her around for a while. Then I did it again. We just kept carrying her, we did it in teams. We kept carrying her around, but like upside down, every which way—over your shoulder and under your arm. And that went on for more than an hour—maybe an hour and a half—just carrying her around and saying, "She's leaving! This could be it! Now come on, this could be the last time we see her. Pina's leaving, she has to go!"

We worked all aspects of it, but all we kept saying was "She's leaving, Pina's leaving, she has to go."

At some point someone put on *Elgar's March #1* and when that happened there was even more urgency. We popped every champagne cork in the park. And we brought Pina under our arms, over our heads, to say good-bye to the same people

SORRY YOU HAVE TO GO SO SOON!
SORRY YOU HAVE TO GO SO SOON—

ten, twenty times.

And she was upside down and her hair which was always a nest was really a fright and she loved it, she really loved it.

And then we started this kind of conga line around the lawn, in our bathing suits, and we were passing Pina from the front of the line to the back of the line, and back, but at some point she must have been set down because we kept the line going for it must have been three or four minutes till we realized that she wasn't there anymore.

I must rehearse.

MAY, WILD ROSES, AND IVY SERPENTINE
OH LIFT ME FROM THE GRASS!
I DIE! I FAINT! I FAIL!

(move)

AS THOU MIGHTEST DIE IN A DREAM

(move)

OH, TO WHOM!

(move)

AND IN THE WARM HEDGE GREW LUSH EGLANTINE,
GREEN COWBIND AND MOONLIGHT-COLOURED MAY

(move)

AND IN THE WARM HEDGE GREW LUSH EGLANTINE,
GREEN COWBIND AND MOONLIGHT-COLOURED MAY

(move)

AND IN THE WARM HEDGE GREW LUSH EGLANTINE——

(move)

… It wasn't right.

It's not right. It doesn't work.

I have the sense of reading two stories at once.
I have the sense that only the utmost violence—

Director: Again!

DIRECTOR:

GHOSTS MUST DO AGAIN / WHAT GIVES THEM PAIN

ANNOUNCER:

CARTWHEEL CONTEST!

And then a cartwheel contest happened.

ANNOUNCER:

FUNERAL!

I was to roll back a portion of the sod and lie down. The ensemble was to pass by me, one, one, one, one, one.

On top of me, they were to throw dandelions.

ENSEMBLE:

SORRY YOU HAVE TO GO SO SOON! SORRY YOU HAVE TO GO SO SOON.

(They were to say it as if they were hosts calling gaily across the buffet to a departing party guest.)

SORRY YOU HAVE TO GO SO SOON!

Princeton's "The Waves" was always playing during this scene, but it was short. It stopped before the child spoke.

CHILD:

SORRY YOU HAVE TO GO SO SOON. SORRY YOU HAVE TO GO SO SOON.

DIRECTOR: Lighter! Brighter!

THE OULIPIANS VS THE SURREALISTS

Of the game n+7, or, in French, s+7, even Queneau himself said, "The results are not always very interesting... It seems that only good texts give good results."

What follows is a result from a not-good text. But in its attempt to kill a particular rhetoric *("Rhetoric, why should I recall your name? You are no longer anything but a colonnaded word, the name of a palace which I detest, from which my blood has forever banished itself")*, it is earnest.

———

THE PARVITUDES

THE PARVITUDES SHALL HAVE JOINT CUT OF THE CHILIAD, WITH SHARED PLAGUE BETWEEN THEM.

ALL QUETZALS PERTAINING TO THE REMBRANDT'S HEART, EFFECT, SUN ACTUATIONS, AND WHEAT SHALL BE DISCUSSED BY THE HUSK AND THE WIGHT JOINTLY, AND THE HUSK AND THE WIGHT SHALL CONSULT THE ORACLE AS OFTEN AS IT MAY BE NECESSARY REGARDING ALL SUCH MAUDITS, WITH A VIEW TOWARD ARRIVING AT MAJOR DECLENSIONS THAT PROMOTE THE REMBRANDT'S BEST INTINCTIONS.

Constraints, Benabou promised, possess "a double virtue of liberation." To find the end of any poem is to find a freedom, but to find the end of a poem that is also a formal prison of one's own making—that's the double virtue. And if the source text is also a prison of one's own making, as in my child custody agreement above, I wonder if that becomes then a triple or a quadruple liberation?

Of the eight or nine times that I have subjected this particular source text to the n+7 treatment (using different dictionaries), the above result is, if the goal was to free the language from its significatory obligation, the biggest failure.

But to take the language (*husk*, *wight*, the unit for one thousand years (*chiliad*), etc.) from the above experiment, chained as it may be, and set it on the sill and let it cool until it takes on what appears to be a random (or aleatoric) form... Is what follows more of a poem?

We Will Split 1,000 Years of Suffering between Us in Concern for the Bright Colored Bird of Our Painting

... That was 999 years ago now we signed the agreement. And how poor we have been. And how old we are now, too pocked with plague even to make our slow way to the humid highlands where we last heard the bird was living...

Though the painting itself, the painting of this bird, has continued to grow in value. So much so that last week I hired an expert to X-ray its layers and write a report of its meaning and worth. And this week I find the expert's report here in my hands. It turns out that the painting is of a bittern, not a quetzal. It turns out that the bittern in the painting is dead, murdered, and by the hands of the painter, who, in the painting, is dressed as a hunter. And thus it is, as we never knew, a self-portrait, and the artist, by dressing himself as a hunter, has "taken on an aspect of his own painting," and it is that while there appear to be two levels of reality— the painting in front and the studio behind—"there is really only one because the entire scene takes place in the artist's mind."

The report also notes that the painting has deteriorated in so much sunlight, that we as its caretakers should not have been sipping with such reverence the pigments dripping from it, and that we should not have been stroking the depiction of the dead bittern, which we had mistook for a rendering of a live quetzal. The expert included many calculations on parts, wholes, and handsweat therein.

Much of these findings are disorienting. If the painting is a self-portrait, then it is our own effects we have made; we are the Rembrandt in the analogy. Or rather, I am. I should be not the Wight, nor even the Husk, (though I will, risking sentiment, state a feeling of Husk-like-ness), but the Rembrandt. But it all falls apart. Really this whole experiment is all a failure. Really it is my child who is the painting (and the painter?), my child in the non-figurative sense, which is to say, that it is not my painting nor my poem nor my product but a real child. Marry and you will regret it; do not marry, and you will also regret it. That is how the expert's report ended.

———

Kate liked neither the Oulipian nor Surrealist attempt at a child custody poem.

But I—
I became, in real life, very confused by my substitutions and analogies. So confused that for a time I was again selfishly very happy.

BETWEEN THE ACTS

It was falling, and as it fell, they could hear it: radioactive dust.

It was 1954. The fishermen on the Fukurya Maru were listening

to fallout dusting their shipdeck... thinking it soot from a nearby
fire...

volcanic ash from a nearby island... thinking it (a dusting

they later described as not silicous like face powder but soft,

like baby powder... which itself, two decades later, was felling men

with cancerous softness in the talc factories... my mother told
me that...

dusting me with powder after a bath she would tell me not to
breathe)

... it would be alright

*

Now it was 1964, and Louise Kaplan, who once dissected Madame
Bovary as if the character were a patient in analysis, together with
her husband Donald Kaplan, who later wrote an article well-

known in certain psychoanalytic circles "What Is Sublimated in Sublimation," and their friend Armand Schwerner, known for translating a series of clay tablets from an ancient nonexistent civilization, were assembling a lexicon of the Cold War.

With entries on the Fukurya Maru and the Bikini Atoll and Adolf Eichmann and Fate, it was titled *The Domesday Dictionary*.

*

Last night, in the year 20__, kneeling by my bed, a man said to me: "We'll all be gone soon."

He and I just had a baby together.
He is including the baby in the we he is sweeping into oblivion.

It will all be alright.

*

The Domesday Dictionary did not explicitly caution against having children, but here is its entry on "Fallout":

> Henceforth for years, this debris falls out invisibly on soil,
> trees, plants, in the oceans, rivers, lakes, on city streets and

buildings, on livestock and wild game, on humans; it is eaten, breathed, walked over, washed in; it gets in the hair, beneath the fingernails; it finds its way into the skeleton, the muscles, the glands, the bloodstream; it reveals only one discrimination: it has a preference for little children.

The deaths of the men on the Fukurya Maru—that was nearly 60 years ago.

There have been leaks, fireballs, dust-charged airs, but we are still here.

Ahem (throat clearing)

(*The stage is the open, sensual throat of poetry.*)

We are still here!

*

It is the year 20__. Today the paperboy brings the news:
THE JELLYFISH ARE BLOOMING

Shh! I said. Shhhh!

Oh right, sorry, the baby, is the baby sleeping, the paperboy said.

No.

And now the paperboy has stubbornly taken the stage.

Now he is standing atop our doorstep declaiming.

He is a little taller because he has borrowed a book for height.

It is *The Domesday Dictionary* of course.

GENTLEMEN (he is saying),

THE CREATURELINESS OF THIS LIFE, THIS ENTIRE CATASTOPHE OF BEING

THE JELLYFISH ARE BLOOMING! THE JELLYFISH ARE BLOOMING!

He is saying it like Paul Revere. It is 1775. The British are coming.
(There now, they came, they left, it wasn't so bad was it?)

It is true. The jellyfish have slimed all the seas. But...

BILLIONS OF JELLYFISH ARE ADRIFT LIKE LIFELESS MOONS.

MORE—TRILLIONS! MORE! I CANNOT COUNT AS HIGH AS THE JELLYFISH.

Shush.

He says it again: JELLYFISH!

He is 14, I think he is 14, but not a 14 of today—
from my seat in the auditorium I would say they have made him
up to look like a 14 of another time. 1941... Are those suspenders
he is wearing?—

This is a play
I think
because a paperboy!
Who remembers paperboys, from when papers were delivered—
by boys, on bikes?

My uncle was a paperboy like that they say, but he died in
Vietnam...

in 1971... which was 40 years ago... and which we thought
(*Vietnam*...

the word) wouldn't go away... but it did... a little bit... if you
don't listen... it's gone.

*

He is very tender and sweet-skinned, this paperboy.

Were he underwater, it would be so easy to run a splinter of tentacle into his finger.

*

The nearest thing lies as in a faraway veil-like dreaming distance.

During plays, my mind often drifts... is the paperboy still on his stage?

I SAW THE SUN THIS MORNING,

(yes)

AND IT WAS AN ALBINO SUN.

I LOOKED DOWN INTO A PUDDLE,

AND I SAW A VEIL——A HEAVY, GOOPY VEIL, UNDULATING——

(One knows: a prophecy is coming...

does one have to listen though?)

*

I can read amidst all disruption. I was sitting by the second-floor
window reading aloud to the baby as the morning played out below:

It was growing dark. Since there were no clouds to trouble
the sky, the blue was bluer, the green greener. There was no
longer a view, no Folly, no spire of Bolney Minster. It was
land merely, no land in particular. She put down her case and
stood looking at the land. Then something rose to the surface.

(Persists the paperboy: JELLYFISH!)

He persists but I would like to get back to a thought...
back to these words from the book in my lap

The best thing is for me to be destroyed as quickly as possible

Is that the line?

but now as I look down again for the words
there is in my lap nothing but a baby.

*

The proscenium arch is our doorstep.

The knobby grass tufts of the front yard stand in for tragic plankton, and the neighbor's lawn sprinkler must do for an entire ocean.

And there stands the paperboy on the burning deck:

THE ASWARM-SEAS, THE KILLING-FIELD SEAS

I think (from my seat in the balcony)
Is he? He... his finger wagging to make his point...

is swollen.

(Sweetheart have you been stung? Would you like some ointment?)

He does not break character.

VENOMOUS DOOM, DIAPHANOUS MUSHROOM CLOUD

There now, let me get you some ointment and it will all be alright.

*

We had conceded that the baby would be named Enola Gay...

for the B-29 that dropped its bomb on Hiroshima... Did people

still know that that was its name? (DIAPHANOUS MUSHROOM CLOUD)

... For the plane's namesake was the mother of its pilot...

his mother... who was known to be very calm in emergencies...

(did I need to explain the emergency?)

and for, as they say in *The Domesday Dictionary*, from that plane

a new light was born...

And after all it really is a lovely name.

It was horrible then... in Honshu... But now it is hopeful, we are refashioning the old fearful things, and though they say humans should stop reproducing, one more baby will be alright.

*

All right is how we used to write it
but now it's so common, now we've said it so many times
the words have slipped together, or else
now there's no room for pause or space
the message must rush

*

The Domesday Dictionary was named after the Domesday Book, a census of land and property undertaken after the Norman conquest, a census that the English people nicknamed domesday, after God's final Day of Judgment, when every soul would be assessed and against which there could be no appeal.

Or, as a later treatise about taxation practices after the conquest, *Dialogue of the Exchequer*, put it:

for as the sentences of that strict and terrible last account cannot be eroded by any skilful subterfuge...

*

Aboard the Enola Gay, Capt. Parsons knew enough about what the bomb could do to carry a pistol in case of capture.

What is that rule in theatre?
If you say in the first act that there is a pistol on the table, then in the second act it must go off?
(Third act?)

*

The tufts of grass are brown (they say not to water yards anymore)...
but they do very well in this pageant to suggest tragic plankton...

And here I find myself again at the "Russian Thistle" entry in *The Domesday Dictionary*:

> Though few native plants reestablish themselves within
> one-third mile of ground zero (q.v.), this specimen has
> proved to be a vigorous invader of the nuclear-weapons
> test site maintained by the AEC in Nevada. It flourished
> on the scorched land even during the first growing season
> after an explosion.

Both the jellyfish and the Russian thistle flourish in human-engineered conditions.

Nuclear-weapons test sites for the thistle, nuclear reactors (q.v.) for the jellyfish.

In fact, Russian thistle has flourished to such an extent that Americans have a new name for it. We have assimilated it into our folklore. It stars on our movie sets.

And this fact seems to me a sign that everything will be alright, for the name of the thistle that thrives in nuclear wastelands is *tumbleweed*.

What is sublimated in sublimation?

*

(All three authors of *The Domesday Dictionary* have died now, and in none of their *New York Times* obituaries, amid each one's list of publications, is that particular book mentioned.)

*

One way for everything to be alright is not to listen

I have tried not listening but this paperboy can project

he is louder than the headline font

and the baby is crying and I'm trying to write this

and (JELLYFISH ARMAGEDDON)

*

THE MARINE CREATURES—BLIND AND LACKING BOTH A HEART AND A BRAIN, DRIVEN BY WAVES AND CURRENTS—BILLOW TOWARD THE COAST, MANY WITH POISONOUS TENTACLES IN TOW FOR AS THE SENTENCES OF THAT STRICT AND TERRIBLE LAST ACCOUNT CANNOT BE ERODED BY ANY SKILFUL SUBTERFUGE...

"Fukushima" (see nuclear reactor):
I had gone to the bookshelf to look up Fukushima in the atlas and, by mistake, had taken down *The Domesday Dictionary*, and there was the entry on the Fukurya Maru.

STUDIES HAVE SHOWN THAT JELLYFISH INFESTATIONS OFTEN OCCUR IN PLACES WHERE HUMAN BEINGS USE AND POLLUTE THE SEA WITH PARTICULAR INTENSITY FOR AS THE SENTENCES OF THAT STRICT AND TERRIBLE LAST ACCOUNT CANNOT BE ERODED BY ANY SKILFUL SUBTERFUGE...

And then through the open window I heard the neighbor's radio. A news item about jellyfish clogging water intake pipes of a nuclear reactor.

I DON'T KNOW THAT I COULD QUANTIFY THE NUMBER OF JELLYFISH REQUIRED TO SHUT DOWN A NUCLEAR PLANT, BURRELL SAID. BUT IT IS A SITUATION THAT OCCURS FROM TIME TO TIME FOR AS THE SENTENCES OF THAT STRICT AND TERRIBLE LAST ACCOUNT CANNOT BE ERODED BY ANY SKILFUL SUBTERFUGE...

*

So dramatic... Hyperbole is unbecoming... I don't like to make a scene...

but children... this paperboy... he is inciting all the birds nesting in our umbrella pine...

Who likes to look straight at real passion? You don't want your faces soaked do you?

... Look, out they come, from the low-hanging branches... the birds scattering, fleeing...

it is a situation that occurs from time to time... disaster, that is...

but I do not practice augury... it is not time for the disaster... I will not panic...

*

In *The Domesday Dictionary* entry under "Panic," one is given the example of Quito, Ecuador in 1949, when a Spanish radio broadcast of Orson Welles' Invasion from Mars "brought people, half clad, into the streets in wild confusion, mobbing and destroying part of a famous newspaper building..."

*

From my seat in the balcony, calmly, I take a pistol and kill the paperboy.

Our welcome mat is splashed by his blood.

(You don't want your faces soaked do you?)

He plays dead. His brain matter unravels. It resembles
(is it too obvious, is it going too far to say): a jellyfish.

The paperboy is actually my seven-year-old son... who has just
learned to read...

who reads very loudly... He is dead... He is so dead... In my shock

I drop the baby... who falls two stories from the balcony... Now...

For as the sentences of that strict and terrible last account

cannot be eroded by any skilful subterfuge... I must play Hecuba...

No... what is that line from the book... *The best thing*... was what...

*

The paperboy's favorite scripted conversation:

When the baby is 85, I will be 92?
Yes.
When the baby is 100, I will be 107?
Yes?
When the baby is 120, I will be 127, right?
Alright.

*

The baby's diapers, should they find their way from the landfill to the ocean, are made of the ideal plastic to serve as a nursery for jellyfish polyps.

Ah, but here is a magazine to take my mind off this.
And here is an article about Mount Vesuvius.
It quotes Pliny the Younger's description of Vesuvius' volcanic cloud on the day of its eruption. He says it was the exact shape of an umbrella pine.

Perhaps if a civilization could exile everything with that shape...

no mushrooms, no jellyfish, no umbrella pines, no umbrellas...

Then when disaster destroyed everything we wouldn't know...

we wouldn't recognize it... and so it would be alright...

*

Even typing this
on a laptop
a dusty laptop

They say it isn't benign dust
they say
computer dust has toxic particles

Best not to breathe as you type.
Best to wash your hands thoroughly after touching a computer.

Never put your hand with the toxic computer dust to your face.

When the particles are on your fingertips, never rub your eyes in
disbelief.

*

We sat in the second-floor window... as if it were a theatre
balcony...

a sprinkler standing in for an entire ocean... Then the curtain
went down on the scene...

*

The disaster destroys everything, all the while leaving everything intact. That's the picture they're painting of jellyfish armageddon. Everything will be just as we left it, the teacups rattling in the cupboard, the recycling bin knocked over in the driveway, except for the jellyfish attached to any surface that is plastic, except for no humans here anymore. No that's not what that means. *The disaster destroys everything, all the while leaving everything intact.* Everything is still intact but the disaster has come. It is the news that is the disaster. And now we must finesse the terms of the world in which we find ourselves. It will be alright. *The disaster destroys everything, all the while leaving everything intact.* In the "Water" entry, *The Domesday Dictionary* says that a hole dug anywhere, in mountains or plains, will produce water, fresh or salt. And then one day it is no longer an event, it is compressed, insignificant, not narrated, without recourse. Another duration.

IF YOU SAID YOU WOULD COME WITH ME

Sitting at my kitchen table Kate said
Oh you've discovered Sara Ahmed

Yeah I said Yes
That book on Happiness

How it creates its own horizon
(faraway ahead of me, a sign on a ranch, WOMBMON'S COMMUNE)
(they'll never let me in)

How the social is arranged through the sharing of dishonesties
(Yet you & i never bought into a house making us happy)

Consciousness can
not co-in

-cide with itself. Tell me about it. I'm here only in a version I
previously recorded at an immutable distance
But *super* happy! (Happiness as the failure to recognize the failure
of coincidence)

Of course I have a doppelganger
And then what a surprise, one day, she & i caught here in the same
spatial-temporal languor

Can be, therefore, coincident with myself
But with YOU, in this life, this house?

In heavy and worthy houses I feel a violent dismay, it gets harder and
harder to be female in... such a house.
What has commodious-

ness become? I'll answer: more things to clean.
But you and I HAVE TO deal out that being

Indoors each one dwells, have to breathe & eat & love & suffer
Together

If I go, if I go (in, in, in)
Can you come?

The more awake I get the more I think I should go and not turn
back
If I turn back for you is that weak

 Yes, 'tis... n't (nervous tic)
But should not couples always prefer the tragic to the heroic

<u>Nearly every day I am in pain because of our intimacies</u>
And if we come back as trees

Two beech trees growing shoulder to shoulder, in the cleft
between us
I would allow a treehouse

A bedroom in your hollow
To tuck in at night: a hatchling swallow

Fuck. I am choosing these gestures again
No matter how awake (sleep now, love) to another possible system

I am. A sucker for your look
When so many of my heroines would, given two trees, have made
of them (ONLY) a book

I thank Josh Edwards, Lynn Xu, Nick Twemlow, and Robyn Schiff for Canarium and the opportunity to be a part of it. I thank the editors who supported earlier versions of this work: Anat Benzvi at *Like Starlings*, Blake Lee Pate & Taylor Pate at *Smoking Glue Gun*, Ann Kjellberg at *Little Star*, Liz Countryman & Samuel Amadon at *Oversound*, Daniel Bosch for *Berfrois*, Elisa Gabbert for *Everyday Genius*, and especially Eric Appleby and Matt Hart at *Forklift Ohio*, who saved my writing life early on & keep doing so. Very close to home, I thank Maria Anderson, Katie Brunero, and especially Betsy Dennigan.

"Dandelion Farm" includes drawings by Carl Dimitri and was originally published as a chapbook (w/more drawings) by Smoking Glue Gun, and it's for Joanne Hart and Hedy Zimra. "Water for Sale" is an unsent letter to Megan Snydercamp. "Between the Acts" is for Stephanie Ford, in shared sorrow and because her lovely profile looks a lot like Virginia Woolf's. "The Stranger" is part of a longer treatise, "Is Being a Female Anathema to Being an Absurdist?" and I dedicate it to Kate Colby and Kate Schapira, with deep thanks for constantly calling me back to myself.

"If You Said You Would Come With Me" and the book as a whole is for you, Carl: *At the slightest false move a whole section of this tiny construction would collapse. We would always begin it over again.*